PECULIAR PETS

Potbellied Pigs

by Natalie Lunis

Consultant: Nancy Shepherd, Owner
Pig O' My Heart Potbellies

BEARPORT PUBLISHING

New York, New York

Credits

Cover and Title Page, © Corbis/SuperStock; TOC, © Andrew Penner/iStockphoto; 4, © Juli Lederhaus; 5T, © Juli Lederhaus; 5B, Courtesy of The Hawthorne Hotel, Salem Massachusetts; 6, © Stan Honda/AFP/Getty Images; 7T, © Jeff Greenberg/Omni Photo Communications; 7B, © M. Schulte/Arco Images/Alamy; 8, © Christof Wermter/age fotostock; 9, © Lynn Stone/Animals Animals Enterprises; 10, © WENN/Newscom; 11T, © AP Images/The Richmond Times-Dispatch/Lindy Keast Rodman; 11B, © WENN/Newscom; 12T, © Cherie Cincilla/Shot at Ross Mill Farm; 12B, © Jean Michel Labat/Ardea; 13, © Stan Honda/AFP/Getty Images; 14, © Becky Birkhimer/NAPPA/petpigs.com; 15, © Cherie Cincilla/Shot at Ross Mill Farm; 16L, © Cherie Cincilla/Shot at Ross Mill Farm; 16R, © AP Images/Herald and News/Jaime Valdez; 17T, © Cherie Cincilla/Shot at Ross Mill Farm; 17B, © Mary Odgen/Courtesy of Nancy Shepherd; 18, © Nancy Shepherd; 19, © Cherie Cincilla/Shot at Ross Mill Farm; 20T, © Jean Michel Labat/Ardea; 20B, © Becky Birkhimer/NAPPA/petpigs.com; 21, © Becky Birkhimer/NAPPA/petpigs.com; 22T, © Jenny Blaney/Courtesy of Becky Birkhimer/NAPPA/petpigs.com; 22B, © Nancy Shepherd; 23, © Becky Birkhimer/NAPPA/petpigs.com.

Publisher: Kenn Goin
Editorial Director: Adam Siegel
Creative Director: Spencer Brinker
Design: Debrah Kaiser
Photo Researcher: Daniella Nilva

Library of Congress Cataloging-in-Publication Data

Lunis, Natalie.
  Potbellied pigs / by Natalie Lunis.
      p. cm. — (Peculiar pets)
  Includes bibliographical references and index.
  ISBN-13: 978-1-59716-862-5 (library binding)
  ISBN-10: 1-59716-862-9 (library binding)
  1. Potbellied pig—Juvenile literature. I. Title.

SF393.P74L86 2010
636.4'85—dc22

2009016980

For more information, write to Bearport Publishing Company, Inc., 101 Fifth Avenue, Suite 6R, New York, New York 10003. Printed in the United States of America.

10 9 8 7 6 5 4 3 2 1

Contents

A Surprising Guest

Few things could surprise Juli Lederhaus. As a hotel manager in Salem, Massachusetts, she had met people from all over the United States. Yet she had never seen a guest like the one who came into the lobby one afternoon in August of 2008. This guest was a pig—a real pig.

This unusual visitor stayed ▼ with her owners at the Hawthorne Hotel in 2008.

Salem's latest visitor was no farm animal, though. Instead, she was a family pet. Her name was Olivia, and she was a three-and-a-half-month-old potbellied pig. Olivia and her owners had arrived from Rhode Island for a short vacation. For the next few days, they would stay in the hotel and tour the town together.

Olivia with two of her owners, Sean and Keegan

The Hawthorne Hotel, where Juli works, is "pet-friendly." Usually, that means that people can bring a dog or a cat to stay with them—not a pig.

▲ The Hawthorne Hotel

Mini-Pigs

Potbellied pigs like Olivia are also called Vietnamese potbellied pigs and **miniature** pet pigs. These longer names tell something about their size and where they came from.

In 1985, a zookeeper in Canada **imported** 16 potbellied pigs from Vietnam. The **offspring** from these pigs were placed in zoos in the United States. Some of the people who saw them thought they would make good pets. Why?

Where Potbellied Pigs Came From

◀ Otis is a potbellied pig that lives at the Central Park Zoo in New York City.

When fully grown, potbellied pigs weigh only from 60 to 175 pounds (27 to 79 kg) and measure about two feet (.6 m) high at the shoulder. A farm pig, however, weighs at least 600 pounds (272 kg) and can be at least three feet (1 m) high. Potbellied pigs are sized more like medium-size dogs than hogs—just the right size for a pet.

This potbellied pig lives with two dogs in New Jersey.

Farmers use the word *hog* to mean a large farm pig. The biggest ones can weigh more than 1,000 pounds (454 kg).

7

Small, Smart, and Social

Potbellied pigs are small enough to fit in a dog bed or in a car. However, that's not the only reason people think they make good pets. The pint-size pigs are also very smart and very **social**.

▲ Pigs enjoy playing together. When they are happy, they wag their tails—just like dogs.

Like other kinds of pigs, potbellied pigs normally live in groups called **herds**. The members of a herd carefully observe and learn from one another. They also use snorts, grunts, and squeals to "talk" to each other. The different noises they make have different meanings. For example, one sound means "I'm hungry!" Another means "I'm scared!" Still another means "I'm happy to see you!"

Many scientists think that pigs are smarter than dogs.

One of the most common potbellied pig sounds is *"ouff."* It is a greeting that means "Hello, I'm glad you have come to spend time with me."

Tricks for Treats

Potbellied pigs are good learners. They can be taught their names in just a few days—which means they also learn to come when they are called. That's not the only important "pet" skill that owners teach them, though. The little pigs can learn to walk on a leash. They can be **housebroken** so that they wait until they are outdoors to go to the bathroom. Many also learn fun tricks such as jumping over small **hurdles** or playing a toy piano.

Horses aren't the only animals that can jump over objects.

Not surprisingly, the key to training a potbellied pig is food. Owners give their pets small treats whenever they get things right. Before long, the smart little animals learn that it pays to be good!

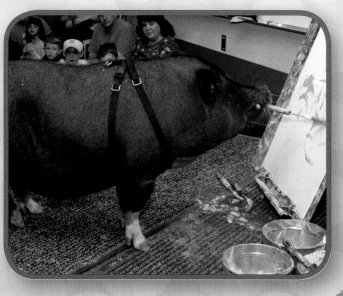

▲ Some potbellied pigs can be taught to paint.

Raisins, grapes, and popcorn are some of the treats that people use to help train potbellied pigs.

This potbellied pig ▶ has learned to ride a skateboard.

Eating Like a Pig

Besides treats used during training, what do potbellied pigs eat? Most owners feed their pets a meal of potbellied pig food twice a day. This "pig chow" contains most of the **protein** and other **nutrients** that the animals need.

▲ Potbellied pigs are not fussy eaters.

Baby pigs are fed a special food ▶ made for their needs—just like puppies are fed "puppy food."

For even more healthy eating, pet pigs should also get a mixture of fresh vegetables with each meal. This side dish of "salad" can be made up of pieces of potatoes, carrots, and lettuce.

This potbellied pig is eating its veggies.

Owners have to be careful not to let their pets "pig out" and eat whatever they want. If they do, the pigs could gain too much weight.

Indoor Living

Unlike farm pigs, potbellied pigs can feel at home indoors. They can even be trained to use a **litter box**, just like a cat. Of course, a potbellied pig's litter box has to be bigger than a cat's. That's because the container needs to have enough room for the pig to turn around.

Since pet pigs might try to eat kitty litter—which is made from clay—people often use newspaper as "piggy litter" instead.

▲ Potbellied pigs enjoy hanging out indoors.

Owners who allow their pigs to spend some time indoors need to do more than just housebreak or litter-train their pets. They also need to "pig-proof" their houses. Pigs bring their habit of **rooting**—using their snouts to dig around for roots, worms, and other tasty things—indoors. So their owners need to hide items that could be dangerous, such as scissors, electrical cords, soap, and plastic bags.

Many owners put up gates to keep their pigs out of some rooms. That way, they have to pig-proof only part of their homes.

Outdoor Living

Potbellied pigs enjoy hanging out indoors, but they enjoy being outdoors, too. In fact, a pet pig is in "hog heaven" in a grassy yard, since it can root around as much as it wants. It can also **graze**, munching on tasty grass.

◄ When a pig does a lot of grazing, its owner should cut down on the amount of pig chow it gets.

Many potbellied pig owners add ▶ indoor/outdoor "dog doors" to their homes. This way, their pets have the best of both worlds.

16

To stay safe and comfortable outdoors, pet pigs need a couple of extra items in their yards. They need a hut or other shelter so that they can go in and stay warm on cold days. On hot days, they need a small pool filled with a few inches of water. Pigs cannot sweat to cool off, so lying or rolling around in the water helps keep them from overheating.

A pig's skin gets sunburned easily, so it needs shade as well as shelter in its yard.

Many people think of pigs as dirty animals because they roll in mud—but this idea is incorrect. Pigs don't roll in mud because they want to be dirty. They roll in mud to cool themselves off and protect their skin from the sun.

▲ Pigs enjoy cooling off in a small pool.

17

A "Pig" Responsibility

People have been keeping potbellied pigs as pets in the United States only since the 1980s. During this time, many new owners have run into problems or changed their minds regarding their pets.

Before getting a pet pig, it is important to find out if there is a **veterinarian** nearby who can take care of the pig's medical needs.

▲ A vet is making sure this potbellied pig is healthy.

For example, some people learn that their city or town does not allow pet pigs. Others discover that taking care of a pig takes more time and effort than they expected. A potbellied pig can live up to 15 years or more, so owning one is a big **responsibility**—one that lasts a long time!

▲ A pet pig owner should have a big fenced-in yard so that the animal can safely eat, play, and rest outside.

The Right Pet for You?

Potbellied pigs are unusual pets, and they bring up unusual challenges for their owners. For example, because they are so smart, they also get bored easily. A bored pig can dig, chew, and make a real mess—especially inside a house. Pet pigs also become very attached to their owners, which means they can become unhappy if they are left alone even for a little while.

▲ Potbellied pigs enjoy spending time with their owners.

A potbellied pig can get into ▶ trouble if it is left alone.

Owners need to be aware of these and other possible problems. They must also be willing to provide their pets with plenty of time, training, and attention. If they are, they will be rewarded with a pet that is cute, clean, and clever—and one that "hogs" all the attention wherever it goes!

People who are thinking about getting a pet pig might first want to volunteer at a pig **sanctuary**. That way, they can learn about the animal and its needs.

Potbellied Pigs at a Glance

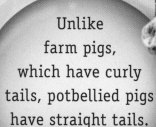

Unlike farm pigs, which have curly tails, potbellied pigs have straight tails.

Fast Facts

Weight: from about 60–175 pounds (27–79 kg)

Height at Shoulder: 13–26 inches (33–66 cm)

Colors: black, white, or silver-gray; also white or silver-gray with black patches or black with white patches

Life Span: 10–15 years; sometimes longer

Personality: friendly, smart, and curious; likes to root, or dig around with its snout; makes sounds to "talk" to other pigs or to people

Glossary

graze (GRAYZ) to feed on grass

herds (HURDZ) groups of animals, such as horses, sheep, or pigs

housebroken (HOUSS-BROHK-uhn) trained to go to the bathroom outdoors

hurdles (HURD-uhlz) fence-like objects that are set up to be jumped over

imported (im-PORT-id) brought from one country to another

litter box (LIT-ur BOKS) a box or container that is filled with bits of paper, clay, or wood and is used as a place for an animal to go to the bathroom

miniature (MIN-ee-uh-chur) smaller than usual

nutrients (NOO-tree-uhnts) things that are found in food and needed by animals to stay healthy

offspring (AWF-spring) an animal's young

protein (PROH-teen) a substance found in meat, cheese, eggs, and fish that an animal's body uses to build bone and muscle

responsibility (ri-*spon*-suh-BIL-uh-tee) a job; being in charge of something

rooting (ROOT-ing) when a pig uses its snout to dig around for things found under the ground

sanctuary (SANGK-choo-*er*-ee) a place where animals are cared for and protected

social (SOH-shuhl) living in groups and having contact with others

veterinarian (*vet*-ur-uh-NER-ee-uhn) a doctor who cares for animals

Index

Bibliography

Kelsey-Wood, Dennis. *Pot-Bellied Pigs*. Neptune, NJ: T.F.H. Publications, Inc. (1997).

Mull, Kayla, and Lorrie Blackburn, D.V.M. *Pot-Bellied Pet Pigs: Mini-Pig Care and Training*. Orange, CA: All Publishing (1989).

Storer, Pat. *Pot Bellies and Other Miniature Pigs (A Complete Pet Owner's Manual)*. Hauppauge, NY: Barron's (1992).

Read More

Binns, Tristan Boyer. *Potbellied Pigs (Keeping Unusual Pets)*. Chicago: Heinemann (2004).

Orr, Tamra. *How to Convince Your Parents You Can Care for a Potbellied Pig*. Hockessin, DE: Mitchell Lane Publishers (2009).

Stone, Lynn M. *Pot-Bellied Pigs (Weird Pets)*. Vero Beach, FL: Rourke (2002).

Learn More Online

To learn more about potbellied pigs, visit
www.bearportpublishing.com/PeculiarPets

About the Author

Natalie Lunis has written many nonfiction books for children. She lives in the Hudson River Valley, just north of New York City.